LORD HELP!!!

We Are NOT DOING THAT Or THAT In this Store TODAY!!

Written by Michelle Ingram

AS I pulled into the parking lot of my favorite store, I could hear their thoughts running through their little minds,

I saw their faces in my rearview mirror with anticipation that we're about to have so much fun in this store.

I quickly parked the car then I began to lay down the rules of the do's and don'ts that would begin once we entered the store.

I started with now girls and boys let me begin with we are not doing that are that today in this store so, let me make it clear.

They said what do you mean, we are not

doing that or that?

I began with...

We are not crying, yelling or screaming

Nope we are not doing that

No touching

No fighting

Or

No poking each other

No running or jumping in this store

Nope we are not doing that

No hiding or playing with the items in the store

Nope we are not doing that

No falling out or laying on the floor in this store

Nope we are not doing that

No huffing and puffing because it's not going your way

Nope we are not doing that

Nope we are not doing any of that today!

No talking loud or not responding to me when I call your name

Nope we are not doing that at all today!

Now let me see if you have heard what I said...

They began to say....

No crying

No yelling

No screaming

No touching

No fighting

No poking each other

No running or jumping

No hiding or playing

No falling out

No laying on the floor in the store

No falling out or laying on the floor in this store

Nope we are not doing that

No huffing and puffing because it's not going your way

Nope we are not doing that

No begging and pleading for things you see

Nope we are not doing that

No mad faces or poked out lips

Nope! Nope! Nope!

No huffing or puffing
No begging or pleading for anything we see

No mad faces or poked out lips
Because we can't have what we see?

We can't do anything today?

That's right
Sounds like you got it

I think we are all clear!

But if you happen to forget by the time we hit the store door, I have something in my purse to remind you of the things we are not doing in this store.

Their faces changed as if to say are we really not doing any of that in this store today?

I respond to the sad faces, Nope we are not doing any of that in this store on today!

Proverbs 22:6

Train up a child in the way he should go; And when he is old, he will not depart from it.